TERROR AT SEA

by Anthony Masters
Illustrated by Ian Heard

W

FRANKLIN WATTS

LONDON•SYDNEY

Editor-in-Chief John C. Miles
Designer Jason Billin/Billin Design Solutions
Art Director Jonathan Hair

Cover artwork by Mark Bergin

First published in 2000
by Franklin Watts
96 Leonard Street
London
EC2A 4XD

Franklin Watts Australia
56 O'Riordan Street
Alexandria
NSW 2015

ISBN   0 7496 3724 2 (hbk)
       0 7496 4007 3 (pbk)

Dewey classification: 363.1

A CIP catalogue record for this book is available
from the British Library.

Printed in Great Britain

CONTENTS

SHARK ATTACK

■ CHAPTER ONE

The white-tipped reef shark suddenly appeared. It stared at the famous underwater explorer and scientist, Jacques Cousteau, and swam away. Jacques wasn't worried. White-tipped reef sharks are usually harmless and barely one-and-half metres long. But this shark was not alone.

Another white-tip glided out of a tunnel of coral in the Red Sea – and then more. Within a few minutes Jacques and his fellow diver, Frédéric, had counted a dozen sharks. Soon there were twenty and then thirty. What could be going on? They'd never seen so many sharks in a group before.

The underwater explorers had been taken by surprise. Jacques glanced at Frédéric and they both swam behind an outcrop of coral. The only weapon they had was a 'shark billy'.

Frédéric and a friend had made the billy after a nasty brush with death during a dive in the Atlantic.

The two divers had come face-to-face with a big silver-tip shark, and had only managed to drive the thing away by hitting it on the snout with a camera.

This had given the divers the idea of making a stick about 60 cm long with an iron tip that would drive away a shark without breaking its skin. If blood gets into the water, the smell

excites sharks and they become highly
dangerous.

Now Jacques and Frédéric
wondered why there were so many
sharks around. They guessed there
must be something dead drifting
nearby. Sharks have a strong sense of
smell. They can also feel the slightest
movement in the water. They can
even sense changes in water pressure

created by the breathing of their prey.

The sharks came up to take a look at Jacques and Frédéric. They always attack the weakest prey – the young, the sick or the injured. Luckily, with their flippers and outstretched arms, the divers must have measured at least three metres. They would have looked very big to the sharks.

Jacques and Frédéric thought they might be able to escape – unless one of them got wounded. At the first sign of blood they would have no chance of surviving. The sharks would attack them at once.

■ CHAPTER TWO

Frédéric and Jacques had talked about
the chance of a shark attack ever
since they had started working
together. They had decided they
could explore under water safely if
they each carried a 'shark billy'.

But this time was different. They had never seen so many sharks in one small area before. By now there must have been almost a hundred.

Jacques and Frédéric paddled along the coral slope where they met the other two members of the diving team, Henri and Raymond. They, too, were worried.

The sharks were now following them closely. The divers hit them on their snouts with the shark billies. But the sharks just circled nearer and nearer.

Paddling as fast as they could, the divers crossed an underwater valley. They could see stony corals, delicate sea ferns, moss animals and tube worms as well as shells, crabs, sea urchins and starfish. There were also hundreds of fish of different shapes, sizes and colours. But although this was a very beautiful world, it was also a cruel one. Only the fittest or the best camouflaged of the sea creatures would survive.

A school of young barracudas shot up from the depths. A shoal of angel fish hid in the coral forest. The inhabitants of the reef were disappearing back into their burrows. The sharks were coming – in their hundreds.

■ CHAPTER THREE

When Jacques looked up he could see the reef sharks swimming above his diving team in the clear blue water. But now another type of shark had joined them. A five-metre silver-tip.

The divers tensed. This was even worse. The silver-tip shark is one of the seven types of shark that are most dangerous to human beings. Others are the great white, the blue, the tiger, the sand, the hammerhead and the mako.

The silver-tip was easy to identify. This shark has a pointed snout, a distinctive tail and large pectoral fins that stretch out sideways, like arms.

The silver-tip was looking for food. As it swam to and fro, the shark had its mouth half open, giving the divers a good view of its sharp, pointed teeth. They were so sharp they could slash through a human body in seconds.

SOME DANGEROUS SHARKS

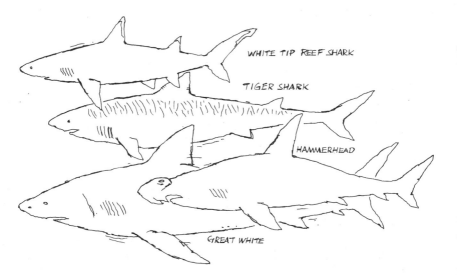

WHITE TIP REEF SHARK

TIGER SHARK

HAMMERHEAD

GREAT WHITE

Frédéric urgently pointed upwards for there was no time to lose. They had to make a quick escape. If the silver-tip smelt the blood that had made the other sharks come to the reef in the first place, then it might attack the divers at any moment.

Jacques knew there was no point in taking a risk by attacking this creature with the billy. Although the weapon might see off the silver-tip, the shark was more likely to become angry.

The four men knew what to do. All divers practise for an emergency like this. They grouped themselves back-to-back in pairs.

Then, as they made for the surface, each diver was tightly locked against his partner, checking out his own view of the sea.

■ CHAPTER FOUR

The five-metre silver-tip was still circling hungrily, certain there was food around. Could the beast be wondering if the 'food' was the strange back-to-back humans hurriedly trying to reach the surface?

Jacques was trying to work out at what stage the silver-tip might make an attack. Most sharks circle a diver, slowly at first and then faster and faster. A diver on his own cannot survive these tactics. In the end the shark will get behind him and go for the kill.

Back-to-back swimming gives a

much better chance. Each diver can keep an eye on the shark, which will think its prey is twice as big.

As the four divers made their way up to the surface, the silver-tip came in close and then swam off again. Jacques felt a sweeping sense of relief. Then he looked down and saw the shark coming up from below.

It began to circle them again.

The divers were three metres from the surface. But they had to stop. If they didn't wait they might get the 'bends'. Nitrogen increases in the body deep under water. It must be given time to leave the body before the surface is reached. If this doesn't happen the diver could seize up.

Squeezing closer together, the divers waited for the attack. None of them had been so afraid of a shark before because they had never been so close.

■ CHAPTER FIVE

Jacques had once faced an two-and-a-half-metre long blue shark when he had gone diving to catch some fish for dinner. He had kept his eyes on the shark by swimming backwards, keeping it at a distance with the muzzle of his speargun.

When Jacques had got an arm's length away, he had heaved himself out of the water on to a rock with a strength that had surprised him.

The shark charged, but a second too late, although it managed to slice through one of Jacques' flippers. Later, he found the half that remained had the mark of a semi-circle of razor-sharp teeth.

Now the four divers watched in horror as the silver-tip shark swam around them in smaller and smaller circles. Worse still, the current was pulling them towards the reef. Soon the divers would reach the big breakers.

Gradually the force of the current began to split up their back-to-back formation. A desperate decision had to be made. Each pair was to split up and all four of them would swim on their own as fast as they could for shallow water. At least – that was the plan.

Jacques couldn't see the shark anywhere.

He was being tossed about by whirlpools and the current itself.

All he could hear was the roaring of the breakers as he was dragged over sharp and painful coral.

Within seconds he was covered in cuts and bruises. He could see his

own pale blood flowing into the
water and knew it would immediately
attract sharks. He wondered what
had happened to his friends. Were
they as battered as he was? And
were they leaking blood into the sea
as well? If so, there would be a mass
attack by the sharks.

For a moment, Jacques panicked, certain that the shark was heading his way, waiting for its sharp teeth to hack him to pieces. He remembered all too clearly what had happened to his flipper.

■ CHAPTER SIX

To their amazement, the breakers threw Jacques and his three friends up on to the safety of the reef.

They got to their feet, laughing nervously. Their cuts were stinging in the salty air, but they felt deeply thankful that they were at last out of reach of the silver-tip.

The expedition member who had been supervising their dive from a dinghy tried to pick them up from the reef. But the boat soon got into trouble and he was thrown ashore by the breakers.

Jacques and his friends quickly

managed to rescue him as well as the dinghy. The silver-tip was not going to have a feast after all!

The divers returned to their main ship. The ship's doctor spent a long time trying to treat and stitch their wounds.

A diver who had not been with them on the reef said to Jacques, 'If only you had taken a camera you could have got some terrific pictures of the five-metre silver-tip.'

Jacques and his friends were not so sure. They had only just escaped with their lives. Even now, they could still remember the shark lazily circling them, waiting to move in for the kill.

TRAPPED ON
THE OCEAN BED

■ CHAPTER ONE

It was May 23rd, 1939.

The submarine *Squalus* had only just been built. She was on sea trials off the coast of New England.

At 0840 hours the captain gave orders to his crew: 'Clear the bridge and secure the hatches for diving.'

A hooter sounded the alert. The crew hurried down below.

The *Squalus* was officially part of the new S Class 2nd Group, weighed

nearly 1,500 tonnes and measured 95 metres from bow to stern.

She carried eight 53-cm torpedo tubes plus a deck-mounted 100-mm gun that could be used when she was on the surface. The *Squalus* was owned by the US Navy. Lieutenant Oliver Naquin was in command, with five officers and a crew of fifty-one.

As the submarine dived, something went wrong.

The sea started to pour in and the engine room flooded. *Squalus* began to sink rapidly. The lights flickered and went out. There was a moment of pitch darkness before the emergency lighting came on.

Fittings, metal tools, china and wooden boxes rattled down the central catwalk. The crew fell over, and as the *Squalus* went into a steeper dive sailors slid down the inside of the submarine. Bleeding, they staggered to their feet and struggled back to their diving stations.

■ CHAPTER TWO

In the forward battery room, blue
flames leaped from terminals. One of
the sailors risked being killed to cut
off the power.

Lieutenant Naquin, the captain of
the *Squalus*, was horrified. 'How?' he
muttered to himself. 'How? What
can have gone so wrong? Has
someone made a mistake? Or is
there some technical fault?'

Squalus was now out of control.
In the end she hit the sea bed.
The submarine was now nearly
75 metres below the surface of
the ocean.

Twenty-six men in the aft section of the *Squalus* died immediately. The other thirty-three were in the forward section and survived.

The water temperature was just above freezing. Inside the submarine there were only a few emergency lights.

The captain carried out an inspection of the *Squalus*. He found that the main induction valve that fed air to the diesel engines had failed.

For some reason that couldn't be explained, the failure hadn't been picked up by the warning lights on the diving control panel. Twenty-three survivors were in the control room and ten in the bow torpedo room. Everyone was terrified.

The captain knew he had to move fast. 'Fire a red flare,' he ordered, and then turned to Lieutenant Nichols. 'Release the forward marker buoy and stand by the telephone,' he told him.

The captain sent five men into the

bow section of the *Squalus* to spread the weight more evenly. No one panicked. The captain handed out gas masks: there was a danger of gas forming in the battery room.

'Move about as little as possible,' the captain told the crew.

Squalus was due to surface at 0940. The captain knew that when she didn't appear a full-scale alert would be called and the search would begin.

The US Navy had five McCann rescue chambers in service. One of these was on board a rescue ship called *Falcon*. She was 320 kilometres away to the south.

The waiting began and the men sat in the darkened hull. They were wrapped in blankets, staring down at the luminous dials of their watches. No one spoke.

WHERE IT HAPPENED – OFF THE EAST COAST OF THE USA

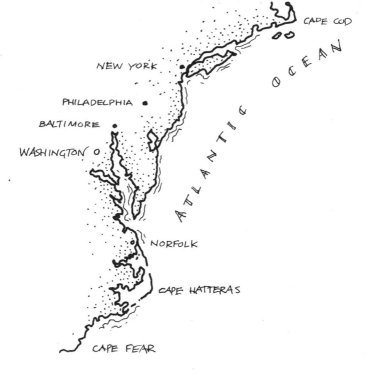

■ CHAPTER THREE

The *Squalus* was now overdue.
Hopefully the search would have
started. The crew wondered if their
families at home knew what had
happened to them. They began to
imagine how horrified they would be.

In fact, *Squalus's* sister submarine,
Sculpin, had already begun the search.
She soon reached the emergency
marker buoy that had been shot to
the surface.

The news of the tragedy had hit
every evening newspaper and radio
station. The deep-sea rescue ship
Falcon was heading towards the

disaster area with a McCann diving bell on board. It had been designed to rescue crew from a sunken vessel. The only problem was that the diving bell had never been used before.

When the *Sculpin* arrived above the sunken *Squalus*, telephone contact was made. An overjoyed Lieutenant Nichols spoke to the *Sculpin's* captain, telling him exactly what had happened.

'We are in 75 metres of water; no

list but eleven degrees up by the bows; heading 150 degrees true. Crew's compartment and both engine rooms flooded. Main induction open. Suggest diver close main induction and attach airlines to blow out flooded spaces.'

But a few moments later the telephone line snapped and *Squalus* was cut off. The darkened world below felt like a tomb.

CHAPTER FOUR

The *Falcon* arrived at 0525 the next morning and divers went on board the *Sculpin* for a briefing. She began the difficult task of anchoring directly over the *Squalus*.

To use the new McCann diving bell it was important to get exactly above the damaged submarine.

The diving bell then began its descent, taking an hour to reach the stranded *Squalus*. One of the operators climbed down through the lower section. He stood on the submarine's escape hatch and pulled back the heavy steel cover.

White, tense faces stared back at him.

'Hi, fellas,' said their rescuer.

The McCann diving bell had just made history.

There was great relief on board the *Squalus*. The sailors cheered. Then the crew realised they were not out of danger yet.

The temperature in the submarine was now close to freezing. The amount of carbon dioxide in the air was rising to dangerous levels, making any kind of clear thinking difficult. Twenty per cent carbon dioxide in the air is lethal.

As the rescue got under way, hot drinks were passed down to the crew. Compressed air was also pumped into the submarine so that the carbon dioxide levels would go down.

The captain had already made a list of how many of the crew could be safely taken off at one time.

As soon as the air inside the submarine was clean, the first seven men scrambled out of the *Squalus*'s hatch.

Then, one by one, they squeezed through the lower part of the rescue bell and entered the upper section.

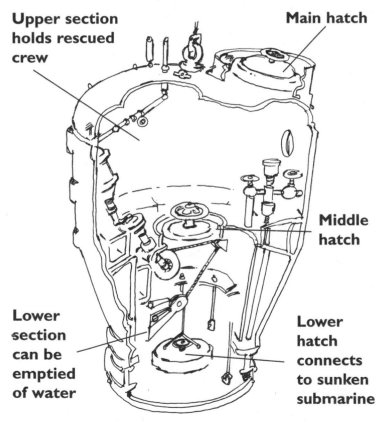

Upper section holds rescued crew

Main hatch

Middle hatch

Lower section can be emptied of water

Lower hatch connects to sunken submarine

McCann diving bell

Here another operator told the crew of the *Squalus* where to sit.

A new kind of tension filled everyone — even the operators of the diving bell. This was a brand new piece of machinery. Would it work?

The operator closed and locked the hatch. Then he joined the survivors in the upper section.

The motor of the cable reel started up and the diving bell began its return journey to the *Falcon*.

Suddenly the clutch of the cable wheel jammed.

■ CHAPTER FIVE

Luckily, the diving bell was almost on the surface. It was winched on board the *Sculpin* while the problem was sorted out.

Meanwhile, in the *Squalus*, another disaster was beginning to unfold. The level of chlorine gas in the battery compartment had suddenly risen. The control room was filling with the deadly stuff.

The captain led the rest of his crew through the gas. Immediately they started to choke. But once in the bow torpedo room they found the air was much cleaner.

The diving bell had now returned and was able to take off another eight survivors. When they were safely on board the *Falcon*, the bell returned. Soon only the captain and his officers were still trapped inside the *Squalus*.

Just before 1900 hours the McCann diving bell was ready for its fourth and final descent.

With the captain and his officers on board, it began moving upwards towards the *Falcon*.

Then, with only 50 metres left to travel to the surface, the bell came to a sudden halt.

The wire had jammed on the reel. Although the operator tried hard to release it, the bell stayed stuck.

There was only one solution. The bell would have to be returned to the ocean bed. A diver would then be sent down to sort out the problem.

The captain and his officers were deeply frustrated. They had waited so long in terrible conditions in the *Squalus*. Now they had to return to the sea bed again.

'We could all end up dead in this diving bell,' someone whispered.

'Rubbish!' said the captain. 'We're getting out of this alive. Somehow.'

■ CHAPTER SIX

The bell was soon back on the bottom of the ocean.

One of the divers was sent down from the *Falcon* to remove the damaged wire.

The bell, with its ten survivors, was now connected to the rescue ship's winch by only one wire.

As the rescue bell started to rise, disaster struck again. The strands of the wire began to come undone.

To everyone's misery, they were again returned to the bottom. The captain told his men not to panic.

'I'm sure they're going to solve the

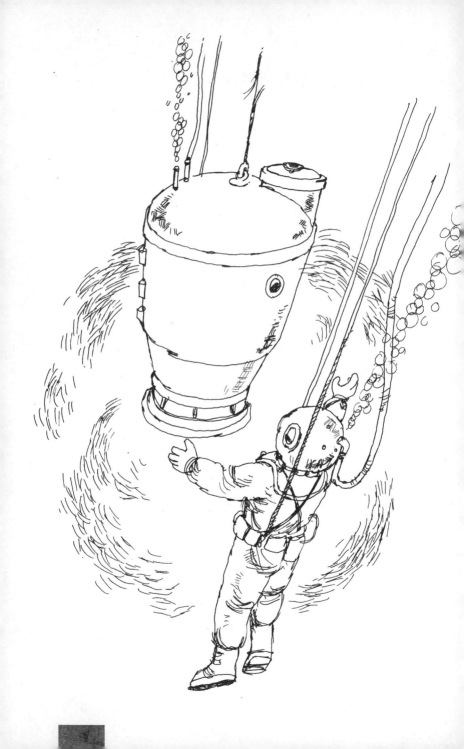

problem,' he said firmly. The captain knew he had to calm them down. But how could he reassure himself?

A second diver was sent down to fix another cable to the bell. But he quickly lost consciousness as a result of nitrogen poisoning and had to be pulled back to the surface.

Again the ten men were now trapped at 70 metres. Yet another diver was sent down. He spent thirty-three minutes on the sea bed trying to fix the cable. But in the end he had to admit he couldn't manage it.

The decision was then taken to pull up the diving bell by hand. This was tense and very tiring work. The team on the *Falcon*'s deck had to slacken the wire each time the ship rose and fell in the swell.

They took twenty minutes to pull the diving bell to the surface, but they did it! The bell appeared in the glare of spotlights at 0023 hours.

The hatch opened and the remaining survivors clambered out on to the deck of the *Falcon*. They were overjoyed but very tired. It was as if the sea had been determined not to let them go.

FIRE DOWN BELOW

◼ CHAPTER ONE

As she walked down the ship's corridor from her cabin, Mrs Loyst noticed two stewards kicking in the door of the ladies' hairdressing salon. Thick smoke belched out from underneath.

She was horrified. There had been so many problems since she and her husband had boarded the cruise ship *Lakonia*.

It was 10.45 pm on a Saturday evening in December 1963, and a dance was being held. But Mrs Loyst had decided to check on her husband who hadn't been feeling well.

As the door of the hairdressing salon fell open, Mrs Loyst saw one of the stewards try to grab at a fire extinguisher. But he couldn't drag the extinguisher free because it was stuck into position with thick layers of paint.

Mrs Loyst ran to her cabin.

'You've got to get dressed,' she told her husband. 'We have one big problem out there.'

When they got back into the corridor they were trapped by clouds of black smoke.

Returning to their cabin, the Loysts found that the porthole wouldn't open because it also was stuck shut with too much paint.

The *Lakonia* should never have gone to sea in the state she was in. A 20,000-tonne ship, she started life as a passenger liner and was made into a troopship in 1940. After the war, she was given a major refit to carry people who wanted to live in Australia.

The *Lakonia* had yet another refit in 1959. She then became a single class cruise ship for round-the-world trips, but at the end of 1962 the ship was taken out of service.

Later, the *Lakonia* was bought by the Great Steam Navigation Company for little more than scrap value. Then she had yet another refit!

As Mr and Mrs Loyst struggled to open the porthole, the smoke was pouring under the door of their cabin. They were sure that soon they wouldn't be able to breathe.

The refit had been poor. The cabins were either too hot or too cold. Some of the showers had no hot water. The stewards' bells didn't work and the bedside lights kept going out.

The *Lakonia* had a lot of woodwork that could easily catch fire. But instead of the usual sprinkler system, she only had fire hydrants and extinguishers.

The problems on board weren't only to do with the refit. When a lifeboat drill was held, both crew and passengers seemed half-hearted.

Everyone was meant to go to their lifeboat stations but few did. Those who did turn up had drinks in their hands. Only a few passengers had their lifejackets checked.

'I can't be bothered with all this,' said one of the passengers. 'We're meant to be on a fun cruise – not a school outing.'

Suddenly the *Lakonia* seemed like an accident waiting to happen.

CHAPTER TWO

After a long struggle, Mr Loyst managed to open the porthole. He and his wife took turns hanging out of it, trying to breathe.

'This is terrible,' said Mr Loyst. 'No one's coming to help us.'

Smoke was now billowing everywhere and the Loysts were beginning to panic. But most of the other passengers didn't understand how dangerous the situation was.

In the dining room, stewards were laying out a cold supper while a fancy dress competition was just coming to an end. Then the thick, black smoke began to creep through the open doors.

The fire was quickly reported to the captain and alarm bells began to sound. But the passengers either thought the bells were part of the fun or a practice for the crew. It didn't occur to the party-goers that fire had got a real grip on the ship.

'The "all clear" will go soon,' said one of the stewards. 'Don't worry.'

But when he closed the bar some people grew uneasy.

Real anxiety began when some of the crew started to roll out hoses.

'Everyone must keep calm,' one of them said.

Passengers from the cabins were

pouring into the dining room in their pyjamas, complaining about the smoke and the fumes. But they didn't seem really worried. They had blind faith that the crew would deal with the fire and soon put it out.

■ CHAPTER THREE

The opening and closing of the cabin doors and portholes fanned the flames. Soon the thick layers of paint on the woodwork began to catch fire.

Captain Zarbis sent out an SOS and turned to his officers. 'Try and reassure the passengers. Some of them are beginning to panic,' he told them.

Most passengers weren't wearing their lifejackets, and confused instructions were given by the crew. As panic spread, everyone on the promenade deck was told to go to the dining room which was three

decks below. There, they found
the fire raging.

The flames and black smoke were
a terrifying sight. The passengers ran
up the stairs again, milling about in
confusion.

Then someone realised a child was
trapped in an outside cabin.

A young steward went over the
side of the *Lakonia* on a rope. He just
managed to pull the boy to safety.

Two other stewards, both wearing
gas masks, also hung over the side on
rope ladders. They worked their way
along the portholes, checking for any
other trapped victims.

The fire-fighting crew put on
helmets, skin-diving goggles and gas

masks, or else they tied wet cloths round their mouths. But they were soon beaten back by the smoke and flames that were getting stronger all the time.

CHAPTER FOUR

Five ships were already on their way to the stricken *Lakonia*. Around midnight, Captain Zarbis gave an order: 'Lower the lifeboats.'

The sea was calm and the night was clear. If all had gone well, then most lives could probably have been saved. But the situation only got worse.

The ship's public address system had broken down and many passengers didn't hear the instructions.

People who had been given seats in the lifeboats on the port side couldn't reach them. Flames had now broken through the deck and were shooting high in the air.

The panic spread and the flames roared. Passengers began to scream. Then a terrible discovery was made.

■ CHAPTER FIVE

Many of the winches that lowered the lifeboats were jammed by yet more layers of paint. That meant some boats couldn't be lowered into the water. Only seventeen of the twenty-four lifeboats managed to get away.

Many of them had to be hammered loose. One passenger saw a member of the crew using an axe to chop a

boat free.

Several lifeboats had far too many people on board. They turned over, hurling everyone into the sea.

Other lifeboats were half empty.

In some boats there was an officer in charge, but in others the passengers had to look after themselves.

Under the stars, the boats floated in the water around the burning ship. People wept and called out for their loved ones.

At least 150 passengers remained on board the *Lakonia*, as well as about 50 crew. They stood helplessly on deck with the flames licking around them. Twinkling fairy lights still lit up the name *Lakonia* between the funnels.

■ CHAPTER SIX

By 1.20 am a huge rescue operation was under way, It was headed up by the British frigate HMS *Montcalm* as well as the Argentinian liner *Salta*. The lifeboats were picked up on their radar. But because there might be people in the water, the decision was made to wait for dawn before going to the rescue.

Back on the *Lakonia*, the fire-fighting team had stopped the fire spreading. The passengers thought they were safer on board the ship than in the boats.

They huddled together on the
aft end of the promenade deck.
A few stood round the piano in the
disco room, attempting to sing
Christmas carols. Seeing the stewards
helping themselves to drinks, some
people joined them.

In the 'Lakonia Room', passengers began to eat the food that hadn't been touched since the fire had started. Gradually they began to feel safer.

'Rescue is on its way,' they said.

Everyone was very relieved. Some people even started to dance.

Captain Zarbis himself appeared in his scorched uniform. 'Everything's going to be all right,' he reassured them.

Suddenly, an explosion shook the decks.

CHAPTER SEVEN

Further explosions followed, forcing everybody to run to the starboard side of the ship.

The wind had risen, making the passengers in the rocking lifeboats seasick as the rescue ships approached.

'Where are the distress flares?' asked one of the crew.

But no one could find any.

Instead, scarves and handkerchiefs were set on fire with cigarette lighters and waved desperately.

Back on the *Lakonia*, panic broke out yet again as more explosions shook the ship. Rope ladders were let down over the sides. Chairs and tables were thrown into the water to act as rafts.

Passengers began to climb down the rope ladders. But when they reached the dark water, most people couldn't bring themselves to jump. A few threw themselves off the deck, breaking their necks as their lifejackets struck the sea, jerking their heads back.

The young steward who had been such a hero before dived in to try and help. He dragged at least three survivors back to ropes hanging from the ship.

As dawn broke, American aircraft

flew over the scene of the disaster,
dropping life rafts and boats.

Only Captain Zarbis and a few of
his crew remained on board.

Meanwhile, HMS *Montcalm* moved
in and began to rescue the survivors
from the boats. She picked up 236
passengers, but some died from cold.
Altogether, 98 passengers and and 30
members of the crew died.

Everyone had terrible memories of flames and smoke and dark sea. The feeling of being trapped – in a cabin, a lifeboat or on deck – gave the survivors, including the Loysts, nightmares for many years to come.

Two tugs struggled to tow the burnt-out vessel to Gibraltar. But the *Lakonia* eventually sank in a gale, taking with her all the evidence about the cause of the fire.

GLOSSARY

aft section the area at the back of a ship.

barracuda a large pike-like fish.

bow section the area at the front of a ship.

cable reel the mechanism for hauling up a cable.

camouflage a colour scheme that conceals identity from an enemy.

carbon dioxide a gas.

coral a hard coloured substance formed by the skeletons of plant-like animals that live and grow on the seabed.

current a flow of water.

distress flare a signalling light similar to firework.

diver someone who swims underwater.

fire extinguisher an implement for putting out a fire.

fire hydrant a connection for attaching a hose to a water main.

flippers rubber attachments for a person's feet to enable them to swim faster underwater.

forward section the area at the front of a ship, behind the bow.

gas mask a covering for the nose and mouth as a protection against breathing in harmful gases.

lifejacket a special jacket to keep a person afloat.

lifeboat station area of a ship where lifeboats are located.

luminous dial a dial that glows in the dark and can be seen without light.

marker buoy a floating marker.

nitrogen a gas

pectoral fins paired fins on the undersides of fishes.

porthole a circular window in the side of a ship.

Red Sea a sea in the Middle East.

refit to repair and repaint.

rescue chamber (McCann diving bell) a specially fitted watertight chamber that contains breathable air and can be lowered underwater.

scientist a person with a specialist knowledge of a particular scientific subject.

sea/ocean bed the bottom of the ocean.

sea trials tests to establish whether or not a ships is fit to go to sea.

sea urchin a sea creature with a spiny shell.

'shark billy' a special stick to keep sharks away.

sprinkler system a fire-fighting device to spread constant showers of water.

stern the rear of a ship.

submarine a ship that can travel underwater.

swell the rise and fall of waves.

torpedo an underwater missile designed to sink enemy ships.

torpedo tube a device from which torpedoes are fired.

troopship a ship used to carry soldiers to war.

whirlpool a strong circular movement of water.

winch a device with a winding mechanism used for raising and lowering heavy objects.

Daring Escapes

Luis knew the main battle was raging in the valley and it would be crazy to go down there.
The bullets thudded around the rocks.
Luis realised he could be hit at any moment.

Read Daring Escapes and find out how ordinary people cheated death in wartime.

GET REAL! GET REAL! GET REAL! GET REAL!

FOOTBALL HEROES

ANTHONY MASTERS

Football Heroes

Cantona always looked very cool. He wore his shirt collar casually turned up and his face showed no interest in what was going on around him. That, of course, was misleading; in fact, he was totally focused.

Read Football Heroes and find out about the thrilling careers of some of the giants of football.

Mountain Horror

*Jon had to get himself going. He had to
make decisions. Above all he needed a plan. If he
slipped off the icy slope he would die at once. But that
would be better than dying slowly on the mountain.*

*Read Mountain Horror and find out how climbers
survived against all the odds.*